BIBLE

Study Journal

GOD IS MY STRENGTH AND POWER

Samuel 22:33

This Journal
Belongs to

Bible Study Journal

Scripture   Date

[Notes & Reflection]

Prayer & Praise   Verse of today

Bible Study Journal

Scripture   Date

[Notes & Reflection]

Prayer & Praise   Verse of today

Bible Study Journal

Scripture   Date

[Notes & Reflection]

Prayer & Praise   Verse of today

Bible Study Journal

Scripture   Date

[Notes & Reflection]

Prayer & Praise

Verse of today

Bible Study Journal

Scripture   Date

[Notes & Reflection]

Prayer & Praise   Verse of today

Bible Study Journal

Scripture   Date

[Notes & Reflection]

Prayer & Praise

Verse of today

Bible Study Journal

Scripture

Date

[Notes & Reflection]

Prayer & Praise

Verse of today

Bible Study Journal

Scripture   Date

[Notes & Reflection]

Prayer & Praise

Verse of today

Bible Study Journal

Scripture   Date

[Notes & Reflection]

Prayer & Praise   Verse of today

Bible Study Journal

Scripture   Date

[Notes & Reflection]

Prayer & Praise   Verse of today

Bible Study Journal

Scripture   Date

[Notes & Reflection]

Prayer & Praise   Verse of today

Bible Study Journal

Scripture   Date

[Notes & Reflection]

Prayer & Praise   Verse of today

Bible Study Journal

Scripture   Date

[Notes & Reflection]

Prayer & Praise

Verse of today

Bible Study Journal

Scripture   Date

[Notes & Reflection]

Prayer & Praise   Verse of today

Bible Study Journal

Scripture   Date

[Notes & Reflection]

Prayer & Praise   Verse of today

Bible Study Journal

Scripture   Date

[Notes & Reflection]

Prayer & Praise   Verse of today

Bible Study Journal

Scripture   Date

[Notes & Reflection]

Prayer & Praise   Verse of today

Bible Study Journal

Scripture   Date

[Notes & Reflection]

Prayer & Praise   Verse of today

Bible Study Journal

Scripture   Date

[Notes & Reflection]

Prayer & Praise   Verse of today

Bible Study Journal

Scripture _______________   Date _______

[Notes & Reflection]

Prayer & Praise

Verse of today

Bible Study Journal

Scripture   Date

[Notes & Reflection]

Prayer & Praise   Verse of today

Bible Study Journal

Scripture __________   Date __________

[Notes & Reflection]

Prayer & Praise

Verse of today

Bible Study Journal

Scripture   Date

[Notes & Reflection]

Prayer & Praise   Verse of today

Bible Study Journal

Scripture   Date

[Notes & Reflection]

Prayer & Praise

Verse of today

Bible Study Journal

Scripture   Date

[Notes & Reflection]

Prayer & Praise   Verse of today

Bible Study Journal

Scripture _______________ Date _______

[Notes & Reflection]

Prayer & Praise

Verse of today

Bible Study Journal

Scripture   Date

[Notes & Reflection]

Prayer & Praise   Verse of today

Bible Study Journal

Scripture   Date

[Notes & Reflection]

Prayer & Praise   Verse of today

Bible Study Journal

Scripture   Date

[Notes & Reflection]

Prayer & Praise   Verse of today

Bible Study Journal

Scripture

Date

[Notes & Reflection]

Prayer & Praise

Verse of today

Bible Study Journal

Scripture ___________________   Date ___________

[Notes & Reflection]

Prayer & Praise

Verse of today

Bible Study Journal

Scripture _______________ Date _______

[Notes & Reflection]

Prayer & Praise

Verse of today

Bible Study Journal

Scripture   Date

[Notes & Reflection]

Prayer & Praise   Verse of today

Bible Study Journal

Scripture _______________   Date _______

[Notes & Reflection]

Prayer & Praise

Verse of today

Bible Study Journal

Scripture _______________   Date _______________

[Notes & Reflection]

____

____

____

____

____

____

____

____

Prayer & Praise

Verse of today

Bible Study Journal

Scripture ____________________   Date ________

[Notes & Reflection]

Prayer & Praise

Verse of today

Bible Study Journal

Scripture   Date

[Notes & Reflection]

Prayer & Praise

Verse of today

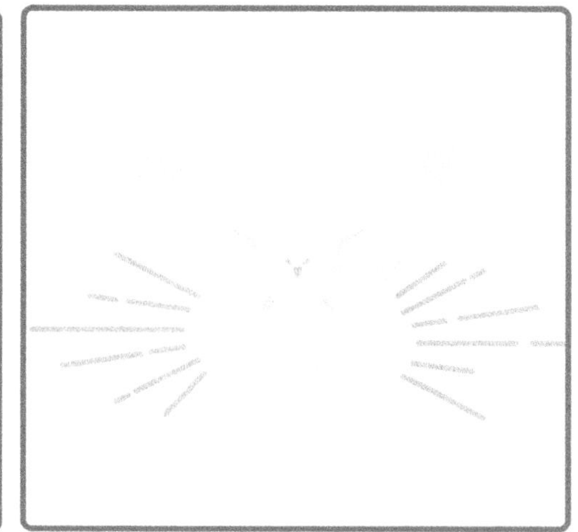

Bible Study Journal

Scripture   Date

[Notes & Reflection]

Prayer & Praise   Verse of today

Bible Study Journal

Scripture   Date

[Notes & Reflection]

Prayer & Praise   Verse of today

Bible Study Journal

Scripture   Date

[Notes & Reflection]

Prayer & Praise   Verse of today

Bible Study Journal

Scripture   Date

[Notes & Reflection]

Prayer & Praise   Verse of today

Bible Study Journal

Scripture   Date

[Notes & Reflection]

Prayer & Praise

Verse of today

Bible Study Journal

Scripture   Date

[Notes & Reflection]

Prayer & Praise   Verse of today

Bible Study Journal

Scripture   Date

[Notes & Reflection]

Prayer & Praise

Verse of today

Bible Study Journal

Scripture   Date

[Notes & Reflection]

Prayer & Praise   Verse of today

Bible Study Journal

Scripture   Date

[Notes & Reflection]

Prayer & Praise   Verse of today

Bible Study Journal

Scripture   Date

[Notes & Reflection]

Prayer & Praise   Verse of today

Bible Study Journal

Scripture   Date

[Notes & Reflection]

Prayer & Praise   Verse of today

Bible Study Journal

Scripture ________________________ Date ________

[Notes & Reflection]

Prayer & Praise

Verse of today

Bible Study Journal

Scripture   Date

[Notes & Reflection]

Prayer & Praise   Verse of today

Bible Study Journal

Scripture   Date

[Notes & Reflection]

Prayer & Praise   Verse of today

Bible Study Journal

Scripture _____________   Date _____

[Notes & Reflection]

Prayer & Praise

Verse of today

Bible Study Journal

Scripture

Date

[Notes & Reflection]

Prayer & Praise

Verse of today

Bible Study Journal

Scripture   Date

[Notes & Reflection]

Prayer & Praise

Verse of today

Bible Study Journal

Scripture

Date

[Notes & Reflection]

Prayer & Praise

Verse of today

Bible Study Journal

Scripture   Date

[Notes & Reflection]

Prayer & Praise

Verse of today

Bible Study Journal

Scripture   Date

[Notes & Reflection]

Prayer & Praise   Verse of today

Bible Study Journal

Scripture ____________________   Date ____________

[Notes & Reflection]

Prayer & Praise

Verse of today

Bible Study Journal

Scripture   Date

[Notes & Reflection]

Prayer & Praise   Verse of today

Bible Study Journal

Scripture   Date

[Notes & Reflection]

Prayer & Praise   Verse of today

Bible Study Journal

Scripture   Date

[Notes & Reflection]

Prayer & Praise   Verse of today

Bible Study Journal

Scripture

Date

[Notes & Reflection]

Prayer & Praise

Verse of today

Bible Study Journal

Scripture   Date

[Notes & Reflection]

Prayer & Praise   Verse of today

Bible Study Journal

Scripture ____________________   Date __________

[Notes & Reflection]

Prayer & Praise

Verse of today

Bible Study Journal

Scripture   Date

[Notes & Reflection]

Prayer & Praise

Verse of today

Bible Study Journal

Scripture _______________   Date __________

[Notes & Reflection]

Prayer & Praise

Verse of today

Bible Study Journal

Scripture   Date

[Notes & Reflection]

Prayer & Praise

Verse of today

Bible Study Journal

Scripture   Date

[Notes & Reflection]

Prayer & Praise   Verse of today

Bible Study Journal

Scripture   Date

[Notes & Reflection]

Prayer & Praise

Verse of today

Bible Study Journal

Scripture   Date

[Notes & Reflection]

Prayer & Praise

Verse of today

Bible Study Journal

Scripture   Date

[Notes & Reflection]

Prayer & Praise   Verse of today

Bible Study Journal

Scripture   Date

[Notes & Reflection]

Prayer & Praise

Verse of today

Bible Study Journal

Scripture   Date

[Notes & Reflection]

Prayer & Praise

Verse of today

Bible Study Journal

Scripture   Date

[Notes & Reflection]

Prayer & Praise   Verse of today

Bible Study Journal

Scripture _______________________   Date _______________

[Notes & Reflection]

Prayer & Praise

Verse of today

Bible Study Journal

Scripture _______________   **Date** _______

[Notes & Reflection]

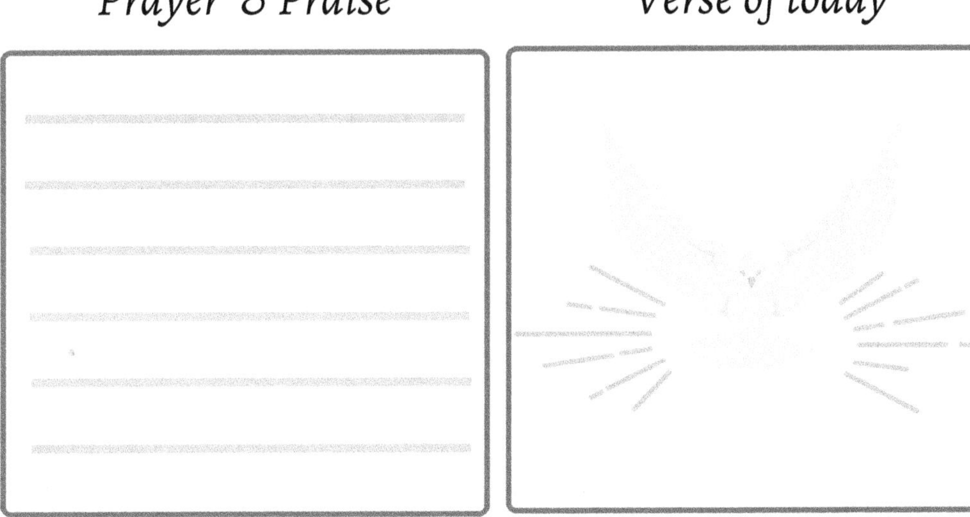

Prayer & Praise

Verse of today

Bible Study Journal

Scripture   Date

[Notes & Reflection]

Prayer & Praise   Verse of today

Bible Study Journal

Scripture

Date

[Notes & Reflection]

Prayer & Praise

Verse of today

Bible Study Journal

Scripture   Date

[Notes & Reflection]

Prayer & Praise   Verse of today

Bible Study Journal

[Notes & Reflection]

Prayer & Praise

Verse of today

Bible Study Journal

Scripture   Date

[Notes & Reflection]

Prayer & Praise   Verse of today

Bible Study Journal

Scripture _______________   Date _______________

[Notes & Reflection]

Prayer & Praise

Verse of today

Bible Study Journal

Scripture   Date

[Notes & Reflection]

Prayer & Praise   Verse of today

Bible Study Journal

Scripture   Date

[Notes & Reflection]

Prayer & Praise   Verse of today

Bible Study Journal

Scripture _______________   Date _______________

[Notes & Reflection]

Prayer & Praise

Verse of today

Bible Study Journal

Scripture _______________   Date _______

[Notes & Reflection]

Prayer & Praise

Verse of today

Bible Study Journal

Scripture   Date

[Notes & Reflection]

Prayer & Praise   Verse of today

Bible Study Journal

Scripture

Date

[Notes & Reflection]

Prayer & Praise

Verse of today

Bible Study Journal

Scripture

Date

[Notes & Reflection]

Prayer & Praise

Verse of today

Bible Study Journal

Scripture   Date

[Notes & Reflection]

Prayer & Praise   Verse of today

Bible Study Journal

Scripture _______________________   Date __________

[Notes & Reflection]

_______________________________   _______________________________

_______________________________   _______________________________

_______________________________   _______________________________

_______________________________   _______________________________

_______________________________   _______________________________

_______________________________   _______________________________

_______________________________   _______________________________

_______________________________   _______________________________

Prayer & Praise

Verse of today

Bible Study Journal

Scripture   Date

[Notes & Reflection]

Prayer & Praise   Verse of today

Bible Study Journal

Scripture   Date

[Notes & Reflection]

Prayer & Praise   Verse of today

Bible Study Journal

Scripture   Date

[Notes & Reflection]

Prayer & Praise

Verse of today

Bible Study Journal

Scripture   Date

[Notes & Reflection]

Prayer & Praise   Verse of today

Bible Study Journal

Scripture ____________________   Date ________

[Notes & Reflection]

Prayer & Praise

Verse of today

Bible Study Journal

Scripture   Date

[Notes & Reflection]

Prayer & Praise   Verse of today

Bible Study Journal

Scripture ________________ Date ________

[Notes & Reflection]

Prayer & Praise

Verse of today

Bible Study Journal

Scripture   Date

[Notes & Reflection]

Prayer & Praise

Verse of today

Bible Study Journal

Scripture _______________   Date _______________

[Notes & Reflection]

Prayer & Praise

Verse of today

Bible Study Journal

Scripture   Date

[Notes & Reflection]

Prayer & Praise   Verse of today

Bible Study Journal

Scripture   Date

[Notes & Reflection]

Prayer & Praise   Verse of today

Bible Study Journal

Scripture   Date

[Notes & Reflection]

Prayer & Praise   Verse of today

Bible Study Journal

Scripture ___________________   Date ___________

[Notes & Reflection]

_______________________________   _______________________________

_______________________________   _______________________________

_______________________________   _______________________________

_______________________________   _______________________________

_______________________________   _______________________________

_______________________________   _______________________________

_______________________________   _______________________________

Prayer & Praise

Verse of today

Bible Study Journal

Scripture   Date

[Notes & Reflection]

Prayer & Praise   Verse of today

Bible Study Journal

Scripture ______________________   Date ________

[Notes & Reflection]

Prayer & Praise

Verse of today

Bible Study Journal

Scripture   Date

[Notes & Reflection]

Prayer & Praise   Verse of today

Bible Study Journal

Scripture   Date

[Notes & Reflection]

Prayer & Praise

Verse of today

Bible Study Journal

Scripture   Date

[Notes & Reflection]

Prayer & Praise

Verse of today

Bible Study Journal

Scripture   Date

[Notes & Reflection]

Prayer & Praise   Verse of today

Bible Study Journal

Scripture

Date

[Notes & Reflection]

Prayer & Praise

Verse of today

Bible Study Journal

Scripture   Date

[Notes & Reflection]

Prayer & Praise   Verse of today

Bible Study Journal

Scripture   Date

[Notes & Reflection]

Prayer & Praise   Verse of today

Bible Study Journal

Scripture ______________________   Date ______________

[Notes & Reflection]

Prayer & Praise

Verse of today

Bible Study Journal

Scripture   Date

[Notes & Reflection]

Prayer & Praise

Verse of today

Bible Study Journal

Scripture   Date

[Notes & Reflection]

Prayer & Praise

Verse of today

Bible Study Journal

Scripture _______________   Date _______________

[Notes & Reflection]

Prayer & Praise

Verse of today

Bible Study Journal

Scripture   Date

[Notes & Reflection]

Prayer & Praise

Verse of today

Bible Study Journal

Scripture   Date

[Notes & Reflection]

Prayer & Praise

Verse of today

Bible Study Journal

Scripture   Date

[Notes & Reflection]

Prayer & Praise   Verse of today

Thank you

for choosing our book.
As a small company,
your feedback
is very important to us.
Let us know how did you like this
book,
at our email address.

 victorpohe.publications@gmail.com

CPSIA information can be obtained
at www.ICGtesting.com
Printed in the USA
BVHW092213300121
599173BV00008B/2824